A loving word
is better than
sweet kolache.

Laskavé slovo lepší
než sladký koláč.

Czech & Slovak Wit & Wisdom

With Great Kolach Recipes from St. Ludmila Parish

Compiled by Pat Martin
Folk Art Illustrations by Marj Nejdl

The Culture Lives	3–5
Czech and Slovak Wit and Wisdom	6–18
Songs	
The National Anthems	19–22
The Prune Song	23–26
For the Young	27–30
Sokol	31–32
St. Ludmila Parish Kolaches	33–35
Czech and Slovak Christmas Customs	36–39
Special Events	40

About the Author

Pat Martin was the first Czech Village Coordinator. In 1977, she began to work with members of Czech Village Association, Czech Heritage Foundation, and Czech Fine Arts (the "museum group.") The Czechs began to fashion their Village, with sidewalkscape, landscaping, building design, and renovations. The City of Cedar Rapids was and still is a partner in all progress made in this Czech community. She has written five books about the culture. Pat is currently active as volunteer with the Guild of NCSML (National Czech & Slovak Museum & Library). She is a museum docent and especially enjoys tours for children. She seeks continually to build partnerships with others interested in preserving their cultural heritage. *Czech & Slovak Wit & Wisdom* is an important contribution to that effort.

About the Artist

Marj Nejdl is a distinguished Czech folk artist noted for her peasant paintings and egg designs. She has demonstrated at the Folk Life Festival of the Smithsonian in Washington, D.C. and has taught nationally.

Acknowledgments

In addition to the contributors listed in this book, we give special thanks to the staff of the National Czech & Slovak Museum & Library, Cedar Rapids, Iowa; and to those who assisted with earlier editions of *Czechoslovak Wit and Wisdom*. Many remembered their ancestors, the Czech and Slovak pioneers came to America.

Editors: Joan Liffring-Zug Bourret, John Johnson, Whitney Pope and Deb Schense. Graphic design by Molly Cook of MACook Design

Books by Mail (Add Postage)
This book $12.95
Czechs Forever $18.95
Czech Proverbs $14.95
Czech Touches $18.95
Decorative Czech Folk Art $12.99
Moravia: Gem of the Czech Republic $35.00
Connected to Place, Landscape Paintings by Fred Easker $38.95
Cherished Czeck Recipes $8.95

Visit www.penfieldbooks.com for a complete list of books, postcards, magnets and bookmarks.
ISBN 978-1932043-54-9   © 2010 Third edition (stapled)
© 2019 Fourth edition reprinted into paperback

The Culture Lives

Bohemia, Moravia and Slovakia have retained identity, language, and culture despite being caught in the cross fire of many wars, their future always dependent on the winners.

Nearly 2,000 years ago the Boii tribes had fought the Roman armies in ancient Gaul, now France. They moved north and east to a new home north of the Danube River. Roman mapmakers identified the area as Boiohemie. The name later became Bohemia.

Slavs from eastern Europe were moving into the area well before A.D. 500. Legend tells that the people became known as Cechs (Czechs) after the Slav leader, Jan Cechus.

Bohemia and Moravia came under the Hapsburg Empire after the Battle of White Mountain in 1620. Slovakia had been under control of Hungary since the Battle of Pressburg in 907. After World War 1, Bohemia, Moravia and Slovakia formed the new free Republic of Czechoslovakia.

This freedom lasted less than a quarter century as Czechoslovakia fell to Nazi Germany at the start of World War II. After the war, there was freedom again briefly and then Czechoslovakia was under communism from 1948 until 1989. Mass demonstrations and a general strike introduced democracy. The Czech and Slovak Republics peacefully divided in 1992 and became independent countries in 1993.

The Czech Character

The Rt. Rev. Msgr. Francis J. Fleming, pastor of St. Olaf Catholic Church, Minneapolis, Minnesota, wrote of the Czechoslovaks: "They have a delightful sense of humor. It is subtle, quick and rollicking. They can laugh from the heels on up.

"This having been said, life for them is no joke. Historically, like other Eastern Europeans, for centuries they have been a conquered people. Travel folder sketches of their history show layer upon layer of foreign influence which has forced itself into their culture.

"Their spirit, however, has never been broken. They have retained their identity, are loyal to their roots, and to this day where two or three Czechs are gathered together, twenty-five other Czechs will soon show up. Stability and dependability are part of Czech character, and communities where Czechs are found are strengthened by both.

"Being hard workers, they love the soil, and raspberries raised by Czechs in their Hopkins, Minnesota, back yards have no equal. Since they work hard for that buck, they spend it judiciously. Both praying and playing are taken seriously, and after a couple of beers at a dance hall, while dancing the schottische (a round dance resembling the polka), one would be well advised to get out of their way."

Father Fleming wrote the above in 1983 for the St. Olaf celebration of the feast of St. Wenceslaus, Czechoslovakia's patron saint. Monsignor Stanley Srnec, pastor of St. Raphael's in Crystal, former pastor of St. Wenceslaus in New Prague, and a native of Veseli, all in Minnesota, presided and preached the homily in English. Czech hymns and music by Antonín Dvořák were featured.

What Is A Czech?

He's everything happy in the world with a smile on his face. He's everything fine in the world with a song in his heart. He is a Czech. He is hope with a laugh on his lips. He's tomorrow with a twinkle in his eye. He is quick to forgive. His eyes dance at the sight of a pretty girl. His feet tap to a pretty tune. His heart sobs at sorrow. Yes. He is a Czech.

A Czech carries a bit of his homeland with him wherever he goes—wherever he stands, that bit of ground is a little bit of Czechoslovakia. He has filtered out from his homeland and carried the secret of happy laughter the length and breadth of the world. He has fought other people's wars, tamed other people's seas. But wherever he has settled, he inoculated his neighbors with his quick laugh and happy heart, and his spirit with a fine capacity of enjoying life.

Compliments of George Jelinek
Ellsworth, Kansas

—The late George Jelinek was a former state representative, teacher, and local historian. He took great pride in his Czech heritage and delighted in giving copies of his "What Is a Czech?" to everyone he met.

Czech and Slovak Wit and Wisdom

The sayings of a people reflect their philosophy.

Distilled over the generations, folk wisdom is highly concentrated in phrasing and in social savvy. Like a native wine, it often has a distinctive flavor. This is the case with Czechoslovak proverbs and sayings.

Lively as a polka, some proverbs show an instinct for playfulness. Others are more hard-edged, showing both a people's refusal to give way to despair and the stubborn perseverance needed to continue.

The history is full of difficult times when the people were impoverished and the country was dominated by waves of conquering armies. But people are survivors. In the face of trouble they cling to the values of optimism, diligence, good health, and education. Above all, they have an enduring spirit. Let's dance, some of their proverbs say. Instead of mourning, let's dance!

Thoughts and experiences handed down to the young from the old through countless generations this is the realm of wit and wisdom. The customs and habits, faults, follies, and childhood games of the people are illustrated in this collection, gathered from contributors in six states.

Friends told of their favorite pieces of wit and wisdom in their own ways. Some chose to share both in Czech and in English, for preserving the language is important. Others, however, chose to translate loosely in English only, believing that in their particular selections too much was changed in translation to make any comparison between languages at all. We have altered the material as minimally as possible, and then only to make the meaning more clear. We present the wisdom and humor to you almost entirely as it was given to us.

For those who chose to translate for our readers, that translation has been difficult. Often the delight of the expression is lost when one does not hear it in the original language, for the sound of the words adds to the essence of many sayings. Furthermore, all expressions are idiomatic, varying according to the areas from which they came. For this reason, we have made no attempt to change spellings and markings for the sake of uniformity.

Our contributors agree unanimously on one point. Whenever the phrase, "as my grandmother used to say," creeps into conversation, lengthy discussions may arise regarding each person's interpretation as it unfolds from his own experiences. And that is the fun of sharing one's philosophy with others… That is the fun of this little book.

So here are the whimsical phrases and harshly practical maxims, the precious, potent words of these people.

Bits of Wit and Wisdom

Food and Drink

Daughters received this bit of teasing if they cried over the peeling of an onion: "Don't cry—you don't have to marry him!"
Neplac vzdyť si ho nemusíš vzít.

Whose bread you eat, sing his song.
Či chleb jídáš toho piseň zpíváš.

When you oversalt the goose, you will appreciate a pitcher of beer.
Když husu přesolíš, žbánek piva oželíš.

Everything has an end, but link sausage has two!
Všecko ma konec, a jaternice dvá!

Toast: Long life to the drinker!
At žije kdo pije!

Eat slowly and question slowly and you will live a long time.

Even the winner of a war suffers from lack of bread.

A humorous version of grace before meals was "Give us this day our daily bread. . . and quick!"

Love and Friendship

A loving word is better than sweet kolache.
Laskavé slovo lepší než sladký koláč.

A good friend is better than gold.
Dobrý přítel lepší než zlato.

Everywhere is good, but home is best.
Všude dobřeale doma nejlépe.

Never judge a person by the coat he wears.
Nikdy nesuď človéka podle kabátu.

Silence is golden; talk is silver.
Mlčeti zlato; mluviti střibro.

You are the fifth wheel on the wagon!
Ty jsi pátý kolo u vozu!

A handful of friends is better than a wagonful of gold.

Never marry an old lady, as she has hands as cold as a frog's.
Marry a young girl, for her hands are warm as a featherbed.

Hope, Despair, and Spiritedness

Time brings roses.
Čas růže přináší.

Morning rain never lasts long.
Ranní déšť neni stalí.

One can get used to anything, even the gallows.
Jeden zvykne na všecko, i na šibenice.

In life sometimes we laugh, sometimes we cry.
V zivoté je nékdy rodost, nékdy pláč.

You are young now, but remember you too will get old.
Mlaď jsi, však pamatuj, ze budeš jednou stár.

Lost time never returns.
Stracený čas se nikdy nevráti.

Better a sparrow in the hand than a pigeon on the roof.
Lepši vrabec v hrsti, než holub na střeše.

Don't praise day before evening.
Nechvál den před večerem.

Hidden things are never lost.
Schované věci se nikdy neztratí.

Enthusiasm itself halves the job.
S chutí do toho, půl hotovo!

Where there is nothing, even death is nothing.

Misfortunes always come in by the door that has been left open for them.

To chide a whiner, one would say (in a whining tone):
"I'd like to sing, but I don't know how.
I would bawl, but I really don't want to.
I would bake kolaches, but I don't have eggs."

Prudence and Honesty

What's in the heart will be on the tongue.
Co na srdci, to na jazýku.

Do not brag of what you do not have.
Co nemáš, stím se nechlub.

He who talks a lot is either lying or boasting.
Kdo mnoho mluví—lže—anebo se chlubi.

A young liar—an old thief.
Mladý lhiř—starý zloděj.

A good conscience is your best asset.
Dobré svědomí lepší než všechno jmění.

It's wrong to make promises.
Sliby jsou chyby.

Well begun, half done.
S chuti do toho, půl hotovo.

Measure twice, cut once.
Dvakrát měř a jednou řez.

What was collected and saved with a teaspoon is now being thrown out with a shovel!

The Material Life

Without work, there are no kolaches.
Bez práci nejsou koláče.

Those who aren't lazy will be in the green!
Komu se ne lení tomu se zelení!

Lazy when young, beggar when old.
Když mladý jsou liní starý žebráci.

The early bird jumps the farthest.
Ranné ptáče dál doskáče.

Everyone cannot have beautiful clothes.
But everyone can be neat and clean.
Nemuže každý krásný oděv míti.
Ale čistě může každý choditi.

A good name is the best inheritance.
Dobré jméno nejlepší dědictví.

Cleanliness must be, even if you don't have money for salt.*
Čistota musí být kdy by na sůl nebylo.

*Historically salt was as important as gold.

Foolishness and Wisdom

If you don't use your head, you'll have to use your feet.
Nemáš v hlavě, musíš to mít v nohach.

I judge you by myself.
Podle sebe soudím tebe.

Fooling around brings tears.
S hračky jsou plačky.

That which you learn in youth is like something newly found in old age.
Co se v mládí naučiš—v stáří jab najdeš.

A horse is only once a colt, but a man is twice a child.
Kůň jednou hříbě, člověk dvakrát dítě.

According to the number of languages you know, that many times you are a man.
Kolik řečí znáš tolikrát jsi člověkem.

No learning falls from heaven.
Žádný učeny z nebe nespad.

Foolish is he who gives, but still more foolish is he who will not accept.
Hloupý ten kdo dává, hloupější ten kdo nebere!

A person who is starting to be a bit of a braggart might be told "*Neházej jsi s kufrem.*" Translated literally, that means "Don't throw your suitcase around." Americans are familiar with this saying as "Don't throw your weight around."

Health

Health is the greatest treasure.
Zdraví nejlepší poklad.

Water is the cheapest medicine.
Voda je nejlacinější lěk.

Happy thoughts are half your health.
Veselý mysl—půl zdraví.

What was not given you from above cannot be bought at an apothecary shop.
Komu není z hůry dáno v apatice nekoupí.

Holidays and Church Feast Days

On St. Simon and Jude Day (Oct. 28) cold begins to crawl from all over.
Šimona a Judi zima leze všudi.

Saint Lucy on her name day (Dec. 13) drinks up the night but doesn't prolong the day. (Meaning that after Saint Lucy's, the nights are long and the days short.)
Svata Lucie noci upie a den nepřidá.

After New Year's Day, each day gets longer by a chicken's step.
Po nový rok, dni jsou delši o slepičí krok.

On Candlemas Day (Feb. 2) the farmer should save half his feed. (Meaning that spring is still a long way off.)
Na hromnice nech si sedláci o půl píce více.

Colorful Expressions

A white horse came to our home, lay down, and covered the whole farmyard. (Meaning a snowfall covered all.)

We rode over frozen pumpkins! (Said of a rough ride.)

He looked around him just as a bull looks at a new fence. (Said of someone looking for a fight.)

If someone says, "I'll remember," and you are sure he or she won't, you say, "Write it on the chimney with a black coal chip!"

Pure exclamations: "He burned his shoes and went barefoot!" "Fifty farmers and one hundred boots!"

When cereal or mush is beginning to boil, one says, "Mr. and Mrs. Chef are raising their hats."

When someone asks, "What are you doing?" a nonsensical answer is, "I'm making a pair of trousers for a stork!"

When a boring person is talking on endlessly, one says, "No matter how long a song is, it's got to end sometime."

Words of Wisdom

Do you know why the lazy man overexerted himself?
He was too lazy to make two trips!
Víš proč se liný strh?
Byl liný jít dvakrát!

—This Czech saying was used when children tried to carry too heavy a load, according to Marie Verbsky, Hillsboro, Wisconsin.

The Professions

One Sunday when my grandfather, Anton Netolicky, visited us at home, the conversation turned to lawyers. "A long time ago I had a friend with several sons," my grandfather said. "He was proud of all of them except for the one who was a lawyer, because that profession was considered disgraceful."

My grandfather then recalled a saying from his youth, back in the early 1900s.

A preacher begs,	*Knéz žebrá,*
A doctor cuts,	*Doktor řeže,*
A lawyer steals.	*Právnik krade.*

—Fern Kaplan Fackler
Cedar Rapids, Iowa

Superstitions

"My mother would never do the laundry between Christmas and New Year's."

"A bird flying into the house meant death, as did dreaming about a body of water."

—Marie K. Vileta
Tama, Iowa

Songs

Every Czech is a musician!
Co Czech to Muzikant!

The National Anthems

The Czech and Slovak National Anthems represent two strong peoples. The music to the Czech National Anthem, "Kde Domov Můj?" (Where Is My Home?) was composed by František San Škroup, and the words were written by Josef Kajetán Tyl. The song lyrically describes the beauty of the homeland and the virtues of the Czech nation.

The Slovak National Anthem, "Nad Tatrou sa Blýská," (Thunder Over the Tatra Mountains), is sung to a traditional Slovak melody. It was written by Janko Matúska to commemorate the exodus of Slovak students from Bratislava in 1843. It symbolically reminds Slovaks to brave any storm of oppression and to stand fast to assure their nation's future.

The Czech Republic National Anthem

Kde Domov Můj?

Words by Josef Kajetán Tyl
(1808–1856)

Music by František San Škroup
(1801–1862)

The Slovak Republic National Anthem

Nad Tatrou sa Blýská

Words by Janko Matúska
(1821–1877)

Traditional Melody

Czech and Slovak National Anthems

Czech National Anthem
Where is My Home?
Kde Domov Můj?

Where is my home, where is my home?
Streams are rushing through the meadows,
Mid the rocks sigh fragrant pine groves,
Orchards decked in Spring's array
Scenes of Paradise portray!
And this land of wondrous beauty
Is the Czech land, home of mine!
Is the Czech land, home of mine!

Slovak National Anthem
Thunder Over the Tatra Mountains
Nad Tatrou sa Blýská

Tatra's filled with fiery lightning and with thunder.
Tatra's filled with fiery lightning and with thunder.
Brothers, let's be daring,
While ahead we're faring,
Slovaks ne'er will sunder.
Brothers, let's be daring,
While ahead we're faring,
Slovaks ne'er will sunder.

Another translation of this part is:
Lightning strikes our mighty Tatra tempest shaken,
Lightning strikes our mighty Tatra tempest shaken.
Stand we fast, friends of mine,
Storms must pass, sun will shine,
Slovaks shall awaken.

The Prune Song

"The Prune Song" is nostalgic and romantic, based on the metaphor of the plum of love turning into the prune of love that has withered. This is a song of young love and rejection, a universal theme of music since the earliest songs and ballads.

To appreciate "The Prune Song," one needs to understand its setting. Plums are traditionally favorite fruits in the Old Country. Farmers often lined private paths and paths to the fields with the pretty plum trees.

Often when plums were ripening, young people guarded them those last few nights before harvest. At that time, the plums hung heavy, bending the boughs of the trees to form a fragrant and luscious archway under the stars.

Charles Seda, retired postmaster in Cedar Rapids, Iowa, had parents from Czechoslovakia who took him back there for two years when he was a boy of nine and ten. On the Seda family farm, aisles of plum trees lined the paths to the fields, and Chuck and his uncle, a teenager, slept under the plum trees the nights just before harvest to guard against thieves, for plums were valuable to sell and to save for kolache and dumpling making, as well as to dry and eat during the long winter months.

For everyone who owned or guarded a plum tree, "The Prune Song" recreates nostalgic and romantic memories of nights under the stars, sometimes including shy encounters such as the one in this song, of young people who spent those few evenings annually, guarding the family plum trees. In that age gone by, these were among the few times that young people were out without adults after dark.

"The Prune Song" is the "national anthem" of the Czech Village in Cedar Rapids. Many non Czech speaking people either learn it phonetically or by this rule of thumb—that you can manage to pronounce almost any Czech word by accenting the first syllable.

The Prune Song
(A Tale of Plums)

Back of our village, on the main highway
Bosensky grows plums—oh yes!
Ann and I watched the plums
We ate them, it was so nice.
Always we sat beside each other.
Upon the stars, we gazed at the heavens.
And now I, I do everything alone.
I think about wanting to be near you.

Chorus: On that avenue
Plums are rolling.
I, today, am not watching.
I, today, am not watching.
My eyes are burning.

Back of our village, on the main highway
Plums are large as a fist—oh yes!
Ann said nothing and ran from me.
I have no desire for happiness.
Ann watches plums with another
Now our plum jam she will not see.
Earlier here stars saw little things
Of which one does not talk.
Chorus repeated.
Back of our village, on the main highway
Plums are gathered oh—yes!
Clothing I have in the wardrobe
And I met with the parson, we have it signed.
Surely after I'm married I'll forget—
Then you, Ann, will remember what you did,
That you deceived me.
Plums now have no value.
Chorus repeated.

For the Young
A Game to Play with Baby

Children receive a great measure of love in Czech families, and much time is spent playing with the baby. One favorite nursery game proceeds like "This Little Piggy," except that it is about a mother mouse who cooks for her five babies.

A mother mouse cooked some mush
In an iron pan. *(stir baby's palm with your index finger)*
She gave some to this one *(shake baby's thumb)*
And some to another *(shake baby's index finger)*
And to one more *(shake middle finger)*
And to another. *(shake fourth finger)*
But to this one *(shake little finger)* she gave none, none, none, none, none.

Vařila myška kašičku
Na zeleném rendlíčku.
Tomu dala
Tomu dala
Tomu dala
Tomu dala
Tomu nedala nic, nic, nic, nic, nic.

Another ending to this game is the following:
And quickly, the mouse ran to hide under baby's arm.
(The storyteller quickly runs her fingers up to tickle the delighted and squirming baby.)

A šup, miška bězela se schovat pod páže.

Riddles

What runs but has no feet and stands still?
A clock.

Who can see behind as well as before?
A blind man.

What has four corners, no feet, and a big belly?
A feather mattress.

Riddle Poem

What is it?	*Co je to?*
Outside it cuckoos	*Venku to kuká*
In spring.	*Na jaře.*
At home it cuckoos	*Doma to kuká*
All year.	*Celý rok.*
What is it?	*Co je to?*
It hangs and knows not where,	*Visí to, a neví kde,*
Points and knows not what way,	*Ukazuje, neví kam,*
It strikes and knows not who,	*Bije to, a neví koho,*
Counts and knows not how many	*Počítá, a neví kolik.*
What is it?	*Co je to?*
Answer:	
A cuckoo clock!	

A Folk Tale

One day a gypsy walking by a priest's house saw a rabbit running across the yard. He caught the rabbit and started away with it when the priest called him back and demanded the rabbit.

"It's mine," the priest said, "because you caught it in my yard!"

"It's mine," said the gypsy, "because I was the one who caught it. If it weren't for me, there wouldn't even be a rabbit to discuss!"

And so an argument began.

The priest suggested that they have a contest, with the winner earning the rabbit. He recommended that they let the matter drop for the next three days, and at the end of that time the one who had had the best dream would win the rabbit.

Three days passed and the gypsy returned to the priest's house. The priest told the gypsy to recount his best dream first, but the gypsy answered, "You are such an educated and respected man that a gypsy should not speak before you do. You should tell yours first."

The priest, flattered, told his dream. "I dreamed I died," he said. "Four angels came down from heaven and laid me on a white sheet. Each angel, then, took hold of a corner and lifted me right straight up to heaven."

The gypsy looked very surprised and said, "Father! I dreamed that very same dream and, since you were dead, I ate the rabbit!"

A Little Bird

When it is winter, when it frosts,
Where will the little bird hide?
I will hide in the steeple.
When winter passes, I will crawl out.

Bude zima bude mraz,
Kam se ptačku kam skováš?
Ja se skovám do vězu.
Až to přejde vylezu.

A Favorite Nursery Rhyme

The dog jumps over the oats
Over the green meadow.
Walking behind him is a hunter
With a feather on his hat.

Skákal pes přes oves
Přes zelenou louku.
Šel za ním myslivec
Péro na klobouku.

Homely Wisdom

"A cousin told me that her aunt, an elderly Czech lady, maintained that a child could be induced to sleep a little more quickly if he or she were given a tablespoon of poppy seeds. I said that the only way this could work was if you asked the child to count them."

—Fem Kaplan Fackler
Cedar Rapids

Sokol

Sokol is the only organization in the United States that originated in the Czech region of Austria-Hungary. Sokol was founded in 1862 by Dr. Miroslav Tyrš and Jindřich Füegner. "Sokol" means "falcon," a bird emblematic of freedom, swiftness, and endurance. Sokol fosters physical fitness, moral soundness, mental alertness, and brotherhood.

Sokol Maxims and Mottos

Your soul enthused, your cheeks aglow, your arms with a lion's might.
Nadšení v duši, v líci žár, lví sílu ve své paži!

Forward, forward; backward not a step.
Ku předu, ku předu; zpátky ni krok.

With a lion's might and a falcon's flight.
Siloulví, vzletem sokolím.

Develop your strength, serve your country.
Paže tuž, vlasti služ.

Your country in your soul, your strength in your willing arms, and courage in your heart.
V duši vlast, v paži sílu, v srdci smělost.

Break in twain, leap across, but never cringe or crawl.
Přelom, přeskoč, nepodlez.

The world moves where might is most applied.
Tám svět se nahne, kam síla se napře.

Liberty, equality, brotherhood.
Volnost, rovnost, bratrství.

Nor gain, nor glory.
Ni zisk, ni sláva.

Either attain or fall, either naught or all.
Buď dospět, nebo padnout, buď všecko, nebo nic.

One for all and all for one.
Jeden za všechny a všichní za jednoho.

With your shield or on your shield.
Se štitem nebo na štitu.

Truth conquers.
Pravda vítězí.

A sound mind in a healthy body.
V zdravém těle zdravý duch.

Let's strive.
Tužme se.

St. Ludmila Parish Kolaches

The Kolache Festival of St. Ludmila Parish in Cedar Rapids, Iowa, is held the second weekend in June. More than 75,000 kolace are baked, sold, and enjoyed at this annual festival.

Kolache Festival Kolache Recipe
Dough:
- 2 packages of dry yeast
- 1 cup warm water (105–115 degrees)
- 1/2 cup sugar
- 1/2 tsp. salt
- 1 cup lard
- 1 cup cold water
- 2 eggs, beaten
- 6 cups flour
- butter, melted, for brushing

In large bowl, dissolve yeast in warm water and add sugar and salt. Melt lard and add cold water to it, then pour into yeast solution. Add beaten eggs and mix well. Stir in 2 cups flour and mix well. Beat in remaining flour 1 cup at a time. When dough becomes too thick to beat with a wooden spoon, turn out on floured board and knead until smooth and silky. Put in greased bowl and cover tightly. Refrigerate 4 or 5 hours or overnight.

Turn dough out onto lightly floured board and divide into 6 large pieces. Roll each of these large pieces into many walnut sized balls. (Another method of forming kolaches is to roll out dough and cut using a 6 ounce size orange juice can.) Grease cookie sheet. Place dough portions on sheet 1-1/2 to 2 inches apart and brush each with butter. Let rise until doubled or warm and bouncy to touch.

Make an indentation in middle of each and fill with one of the following fillings or a favorite of your own; entire dough recipe requires about 2 pounds of filling. Sprinkle topping on filling. Let rise another 20 minutes. Bake at 425º for 12 minutes or until golden brown. Brush kolaches with butter after you take them from the oven. Makes about 5 dozen kolaches.

Poppy Seed Filling:
- 2 cups milk or water (or 1 cup of each)
- 1/2 lb. ground poppy seed
- 3/4 cup sugar
- 1 Tbsp. corn syrup
- 1/4 tsp. salt
- 1/2 tsp. almond extract
- 2 Tbsp. butter
- 1 tsp. vanilla
- 2 graham crackers, crushed

Boil milk or water. Stir in poppy seed. Simmer 20 minutes, stirring frequently and being careful that it doesn't scorch. Add sugar, corn syrup and salt. Simmer a few more minutes. Remove from heat and mix in almond extract, butter, vanilla and graham crackers. Makes enough for 3 dozen kolaches.

Variation: Bakers at St. Ludmila bake in large quantities, so they use poppy butter, which comes in gallon cans. Omit corn syrup and butter if starting with poppy butter.

Prune Filling:
- 1 lb. dried prunes
- 1/2 cup sugar
- 1/2 tsp. cinnamon
- 1/2 tsp. vanilla

Cook prunes in enough water to cover until they are soft. Drain and remove pits. Mash. Add sugar, cinnamon and vanilla. Mix well.

Note: Yields of fillings depend on size of kolaches. The St. Ludmila kolache is largely filling.

Apricot Filling:
1 lb. dried apricots
water
sugar

Soak apricots overnight in enough water to cover. Cook until soft. Drain well of any remaining water. Mash. Add sugar to taste.

Cottage Cheese Filling:
1 lb. dried unsalted cottage cheese
1/2 cup sugar
1 egg yolk
1/2 tsp. cinnamon
3/4 cup light raisins, cooked and drained

Mix together the cottage cheese, sugar and egg yolk. Stir in cinnamon and raisins. Do not prepare until ready to use.

Cherry Filling:
1 qt. frozen cherries, thawed
6 Tbsp. cornstarch
1 cup sugar
1/4 tsp. salt
1/2 tsp. almond extract

Drain juice from cherries into a saucepan; heat. Thicken with cornstarch. Add a little water if mixture becomes too thick. Stir in sugar and salt. Add cherries and almond extract.

Crumb Topping:
1/2 cup sugar
1/2 cup flour
2 Tbsp. butter

Blend sugar, flour and butter until crumbly.

Czech and Slovak Christmas Customs

December 4, St. Barbara's Day, begins the Christmas season. A tradition includes young girls placing a sprig of a blossoming type tree in water indoors. If there are blooms by Christmas, they are considered a token of good luck in finding a husband during the coming year.

December 6 is St. Nicholas's Day, the first celebration of the season. He appears dressed as a bishop descending from heaven on a golden cord with an angel dressed in white. A devil comes along dressed in black with a face painted red. As St. Nicholas (Sv. Mikuláš) walks through the villages, he stops to ask children about their behavior. The angel records the answers in a book and the devil in the background rattles his chains. The angel rewards good children with candy, fruit and cookies in various shapes. The devil gives a lump of coal or a potato to children giving unfavorable answers.

In Slovakia good children who clean their boots and leave them by the front door find treats from St. Nicholas: candies, chocolate figures, mandarin oranges and other fruits, peanuts and sometimes a small toy. Gingerbread cookies in the shapes of the saint, angel and devil are given as well as hearts, birds, fish, deer and other shapes.

December 24, Christmas Eve, is when the fir tree is decorated with a star or steeple top of blown glass, real candles in holders, chains of straw, glass beads or colored paper and hand blown glass ornaments. Other ornaments may be homemade from straw, cloth, baked dough or wood. Ginger and honey cookies hang on the tree, too. A Nativity scene is placed near the tree. Apples and nuts are placed in bowls throughout the house.

Those who fast until the end of Advent may see the "Golden Pig" and have good luck all year. The family gathers around the dinner table and wafers are shared prior to dinner. These flat wafers are embossed with Christmas scenes. They are similar to communion wafers. Others may be rolled into tubes and sprinkled with honey, symbolizing productivity and good health. Garlic is to keep away evil forces and to retain good health.

Dinner may include sauerkraut soup flavored with dried wild mushrooms and dried plums. The upper classes eat fish, turkey and deer. Those poorer eat pond raised carp, which are sold in village streets, purchased live and kept in the bathtub until Christmas Eve. The carp is cut into horseshoe shapes and fried. Christmas potato salad is served with the carp. Desserts include braided sweet bread, poppy seed cakes and kolaches. Presents are opened Christmas Eve.

December 25 is when the family goes to church and has a noon meal, which may include fine chicken noodle soup, fried wiener schnitzel with potato salad or roast duck or goose with dumplings and sauerkraut. In Slovakia men and boys of the village go house to house carrying a miniature Nativity scene, singing carols and bringing wishes for bountiful crops, love, peace and happiness.

December 26, St. Stephen's Day, is a time for children to go caroling and receive treats of candies, fruits and cookies. In Slovakia a dance is held.

On December 31, St. Silvester's Day, a festive drink of eggnog with cognac is served with little sandwiches of Vienna style white bread heaped with potato salad, ham, eggs, sliced pickles, and cheese.

January 6, Three Kings Day, ends the Christmas season with young boys dressed in costumes to represent the kings. They go caroling and are rewarded with treats.

—from the National Czech & Slovak Museum & Library

Editor's Note:
The National Czech & Slovak Museum & Library is the nation's foremost institution of Czech and Slovak history and culture. Dedicated in 1995 by President Bill Clinton, Czech Republic President Václav Havel, and Slovak Republic President Michal Kovác, the museum & library hosts thousands of guests each year, and offers exciting exhibits, a research library, a museum store, and special events throughout the year. Call (319) 362-8500 for more information, or visit www.NCSML.org.

The Christmas Tree and Glass Ornaments

The Christmas tree represents a symbolic ladder to the heavens. Ornaments are hung equal to their symbolic position in life. Vegetables and fruit, closest to earth, hang on the lower third of the tree. Houses, churches, people and animals go in the middle area. Birds and angels hang on the top third, symbolizing closeness to heaven.

Taught by wandering Venetian tradesmen, Bohemian glass blowers first created glass ornaments to decorate fir trees in celebration of the winter solstice. Early Christians adapted this custom from the Dark Ages to their celebration of the birth of Christ. The glass blowers became famous for their beautiful delicate Christmas ornaments and are still using forms over 1,000 years old.

Almost all the ornaments have symbolic meanings. Corn symbolizes prosperity and fertility. A tradition in many families is that whoever first finds a glass pickle hidden on a tree is the first to open a present.

Walnuts are the traditional "fruit" of the Christmas season in central Europe. Fruits once unattainable at Christmas time became decorative symbols on a Christmas tree. Today, fruit is a symbolic gift from St. Nicholas (Sv. Mikuláš), whose feast day is December 6th. The pineapple symbolizes friendship and hospitality.

Houses and churches are symbols of village life. Collectors try to assemble an entire village using ornaments of different houses and churches. Farm animals are traditional symbols of everyday village life.

Birds are symbols of joy and cheerfulness with swans noted for gracefulness. Owls equal wisdom.

Favorite glass ornaments include clowns, carousels and circus animals. In the past, the circus was the main entertainment for the people. Joy and excitement came from watching exotic animals and clowns. The artisans wanted to replicate the same joyous spirit by designing ornaments representing circus life.

—from the National Czech & Slovak Museum & Library

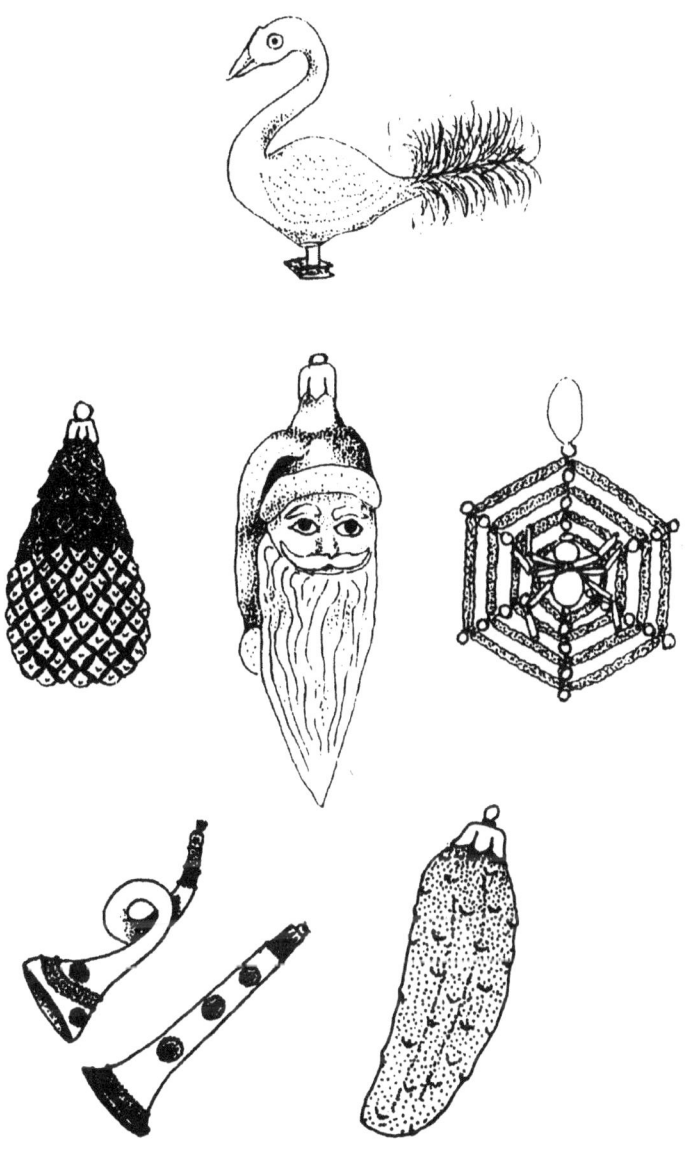

These illustrations by Diane Heusinkveld show six imported traditional glass ornaments by Czech artisans. They include Sv. Mikuláš; a pineapple, spider in a web, and a pickle; musical instruments and a swan.

Special Events

Czech and Slovak groups throughout America have additional events during the year. The Cedar Rapids, Iowa, events listed below may also be held in other Czech and Slovak communities in America. Here is a listing of those special days.

St. Joseph Day, the Czech counterpart of St. Patrick Day, is March 19 and is celebrated the Saturday after that date, in Czech Village... There is a parade and much conviviality. Red is the featured color!

Houby (Mushroom) Days is always the weekend after Mother's Day in May, in Czech Village. We celebrate mushroom hunting along with Czech food, music, dancing, a street fair, and parade. Mushroom hunting trophies are awarded and competition for Czech Royalty for youth is always a highlight.

St. Ludmila Parish Kolach Festival is the second weekend in June. New Bohemia Arts Festival is held the Sunday of Labor Day Weekend, in New Bohemia, across the river from Czech Village. Now the Czech Village/New Bohemia Main Street District is unified. This festival combines music and visual arts.

St. Wenceslaus Parish Czech Goulash Day is held the fourth Sunday in September. Along with a traditional goulash dinner, guests enjoy a Polka Mass and kolace.

BrewNost, an international beer tasting celebration hosted by National Czech & Slovak Museum & Library, customarily is held in September or October. Along with premium beers, it features savory hors d'oeuvres, an Old World Market, Silent Auction, and live music.

Enthusiasm itself halves the job.

S chutí do toho, půl hotovo!

www.ingramcontent.com/pod-product-compliance
Lightning Source LLC
Chambersburg PA
CBHW071953070426
42451CB00009BA/879